Taking Sh

by Marilyn Deen

Consultant:
Adria F. Klein, PhD
California State University, San Bernardino

CAPSTONE PRESS
a capstone imprint

Wonder Readers are published by Capstone Press,
1710 Roe Crest Drive, North Mankato, Minnesota 56003.
www.capstonepub.com

Books published by Capstone Press are manufactured with paper containing at least 10 percent post-consumer waste.

Library of Congress Cataloging-in-Publication Data
Deen, Marilyn.
   Taking shape / Marilyn Deen.—1st ed.
      p. cm.—(Wonder readers)
   Includes index.
   ISBN 978-1-4296-7936-7 (paperback)
   ISBN 978-1-4296-8631-0 (library binding)
   1. Shapes—Juvenile literature. I. Title.
   QA445.5.D438 2012
   516'.15—dc23   2011022025

Summary: Describes and explains the features of flat and solid shapes, including cubes, cylinders, cones, spheres, and pyramids.

Note to Parents and Teachers

The Wonder Readers: Mathematics series supports national mathematics standards. These titles use text structures that support early readers, specifically with a close photo/text match and glossary. Each book is perfectly leveled to support the reader at the right reading level, and the topics are of high interest. Early readers will gain success when they are presented with a book that is of interest to them and is written at the appropriate level.

Printed in the United States of America in North Mankato, Minnesota.
102011   006405CGS12

Table of Contents

Shapes

Everywhere you look, you can find shapes. Look at this picture. See how many shapes you can find. How many circles are there? How many squares and rectangles?

Try to find the shapes on this bike.
There are circles and triangles.
Try to find them all. Some shapes,
like triangles and circles, are flat.

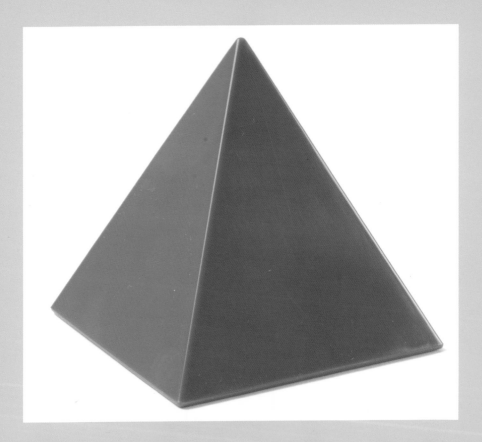

Other shapes take up space. They have several different sides. These are called solid shapes. Each side of a solid shape is called a **face**.

Each face of a solid shape is made up of a flat shape, like a square, a triangle, or a circle. Look at the faces of these solid shapes. The black lines show you the flat shape that is on each face.

Cubes

A **cube** is a solid shape with six sides. Each side, or face, of a cube is square. Dice are cubes.

These ice cubes are also cubes. Each piece of ice has six square sides—at least until they start to melt! Think of some other things that are cubes. You probably have some at home or at school.

Cylinders

Another solid shape is a **cylinder**.
Each end of a cylinder is a circle.
The middle is long, thin, and
round. A garbage can is a cylinder.

The columns on this old building are also cylinders. The middle of each column is long, thin, and round. If you could see the ends of each column, you would see circles. Think of other things that are cylinders.

Cones

A **cone** is another kind of solid shape. One end is a face in the shape of a circle. The other end is a point. The middle of a cone is round and smooth.

There are three cones on this page. The party hats are shaped like cones. Think of other things you use or know about that are shaped like cones.

Spheres

A **sphere** is round like a ball. There are no faces, or sides, on a sphere. There are no corners either.

It is pretty easy to find spheres in any house or school. The spheres in the picture below are good to eat! Try to think of some other kinds of food that are spheres.

Pyramids

A **pyramid** is a solid shape with five faces. The bottom is a square, and each side is a triangle.

How many solid shapes do you see below? Say the name of each shape. Then tell one thing you use or have seen that is the same as each shape in this book.

Glossary

cone   a solid shape with one pointed end and a circular shape at the other end

cube   a six-sided solid shape, made up of squares

cylinder   a circular solid shape that is long and thin

face   each side of a solid shape

pyramid   a solid shape made up of triangles and a square base

sphere   a solid shape that is round

Now Try This!

Look around your classroom or school to find examples of the solid shapes featured in the book. Then play a guessing game. Give clues about an object that is a solid shape, and have your friend guess what it is. For example, "I'm thinking of a six-sided solid shape that I like to put in my water to keep it cold." The answer is ice cube.

Internet Sites

FactHound offers a safe, fun way to find Internet sites related to this book. All of the sites on FactHound have been researched by our staff.

Here's all you do:

Visit *www.facthound.com*

Type in this code: 9781429686310

Check out projects, games and lots more at
www.capstonekids.com

19

Index

Editorial Credits

Maryellen Gregoire, project director; Mary Lindeen, consulting editor; Gene Bentdahl, designer; Sarah Schuette, editor; Wanda Winch, media researcher; Eric Manske, production specialist

Photo Credits

Photos by Capstone Studio: Karon Dubke, except Shutterstock/Dan Breckwoldt, cover

Word Count: **416**   Guided Reading Level: K   Early Intervention Level: **20**